100 Unforgettable Moments in
Pro Football

Bob Italia

ABDO & Daughters
Publishing

Published by Abdo & Daughters, 4940
Viking Drive, Suite 622, Edina,
Minnesota 55435.

Copyright © 1996 by Abdo Consulting
Group, Inc., Pentagon Tower, P.O. Box
36036, Minneapolis, Minnesota 55435
USA. International copyrights
reserved in all countries. No part of
this book may be reproduced in any
form without written permission from
the publisher.

Printed in the United States.

Cover Photo credits: Allsport
Interior Photo credits: Allsport
Wide World Photo

Edited by Paul Joseph

Library of Congress Cataloging-in-Publication Data

Italia, Bob, 1955-
    100 unforgettable moments in pro football / Bob Italia.
        p. cm. — (100 unforgettable moments in sports)
Includes index.
Summary: Describes notable events in the history of pro football.
    ISBN 1-56239-690-0
    1. Football—United States—History—Juvenile literature.
    [1. Football—History.] I. Title. II. Series: Italia, Bob, 1955-
100 unforgettable moments in sports.
GV954.I83 1996
796.332'64'0973--dc20

                                        96-7008
                                          CIP
                                          AC

Contents

The Most Unforgettable Moment?

The National Football League (NFL) has had a long history filled with many unforgettable moments. Who could forget Tom Dempsey's NFL-record 63-yard field goal that beat the astonished Detroit Lions? Or how about Franco Harris' "Immaculate Reception" that earned the Steelers a playoff win over the stunned Oakland Raiders?

Many of the NFL's unforgettable "moments" weren't moments at all. Some of these great feats took a season—or a career—to accomplish, like the Miami Dolphins' perfect season, or Walter Payton's record for career rushing yards.

There is no one most unforgettable moment. The following events are in chronological order, not according to importance. That judgment must be left to professional football fans, whose enthusiasm for the game has made the NFL a national treasure.

Opposite Page:
Chicago Bears' running back Gale Sayers, who scored an NFL record six touchdowns in one game.

The Birth of the NFL

The birth of the NFL can be attributed to its first great running back, Red Grange, an All-American halfback from the University of Illinois. Grange earned his nickname, the "Galloping Ghost," by scoring five touchdowns the first five times he carried the ball for his team against the University of Michigan in 1924. He also scored an amazing thirty-one touchdowns in his three-year college football career. In those three short years, Grange had become a superstar. Now he was ready for professional football.

Chicago Bears' head coach George Halas signed Grange on November 22, 1925, and immediately started a football tour from New York to Los Angeles to show off his new star. The Bears played football in nineteen cities in less than six months. They attracted over 350,000 football fans. Grange had now established professional football as a nationwide success.

Grange played professional football in Chicago for thirteen seasons. But because accurate records were not kept in the 1920s, Grange is not listed among the Bears' top twenty-five all-time rushers. Still, Grange had more impact on professional football than any other player in its long history.

Opposite page:
Red Grange, the Galloping Ghost.

73-0

In 1963, the National Academy of Sports Editors voted the 1940 Chicago Bears as the greatest professional team of all time. It was the 1940 championship game that won them this honor.

That year, the Bears had played the Washington Redskins during the regular season and lost 7-3 on a questionable call. When the Bears protested, the Redskins' owner, George Marshall, told the press that "the Bears were quitters and a bunch of cry babies."

Coach Halas was furious. He tacked up the newspaper article throughout the locker room. Halas then gave an inspirational talk.

"Gentlemen," he said, "this is what the Redskins think of you. I think you're a great football team, the greatest ever assembled. Go out onto the field and prove it."

The Bears destroyed the Redskins 73-0 before 36,000 startled Redskins fans. At one point late in the game, an official asked the Bears not to kick any more extra points. Too many extra-point footballs had been kicked into the stands. The Redskins were down to their last football!

The 1940 championship game was no fluke. The Bears had three future Hall of Famers on their team—Sid Luckman,

Coach George Halas.

George McAfee, and Joe Stydahar. The record seventy-three points still stands today as the most points scored in any NFL regular-season, playoff, or championship game.

Some observers said the Bears played perfectly in that 1940 championship game. But Halas disagreed. He thought his team should have scored more points.

The Best Game Ever?

On December 28, 1958, the New York Giants played the Baltimore Colts in one of the biggest championship games in NFL history. The game became known as the Yankee Stadium Classic—and it would change the fortunes of the NFL forever. The Giants were led by quarterback Charlie Conerly. The Colts had Johnny Unitas, who often threw to stars like Raymond Berry and Lenny Moore.

On game day, rains muddied the field. Each team had many fumbles, interceptions, and missed field goals. Despite the sloppy play, the game's outcome wouldn't be decided until the very end. With 3 minutes remaining, the Giants led 17-14. But then Johnny Unitas drove the Colts seventy-three yards. The Giants defense stiffened, and the drive stalled. Baltimore settled for a Lou Michels field goal which sent the game into sudden death overtime.

Baltimore got the ball and began another long drive. On the one-yard-line, the Giants' defense prepared for a pass play. But fullback Alan Ameche burst over the goal line for the game-winning touchdown and a 23-17 championship victory.

All the excitement was witnessed by football fans across the country, for the game was one of the first to be televised. Having given the television audience such a dramatic contest, the NFL won millions of new fans. Professional football was now a national treasure.

Baltimore Colts' fullback Alan Ameche bursts through a big hole in the Giants' line to score the game-winning touchdown.

Jim Brown
Makes History

In 1957, the Cleveland Browns drafted Syracuse University running back Jim Brown. The 6-foot, 228-pound Brown became an instant star. Not only was he one of the biggest fullbacks in the league, he was one of the fastest and strongest. When he could not run around defenders, Brown would run over them. To stop the Browns, defenses had to stop Jim Brown. It was not an easy task. Brown seemed indestructible. And he was the NFL's leading rusher nearly every season he played.

In 1964, the Browns set their sights on a championship. Along with Brown's running game, Cleveland had an explosive passing attack. Quarterback Frank Ryan often threw to two outstanding receivers, Gary Collins and Paul Warfield. Defensive end Doug Atkins anchored the rock-solid defense.

The Browns were in first place most of the season. But losses to the St. Louis Cardinals hurt Cleveland's title chances. The Browns regrouped just in time to win their final game of the regular season, a 52-20 thrashing of the New York Giants. The victory earned Cleveland the Eastern Division title.

The Browns faced the Baltimore Colts in the championship game at Cleveland. The game was scoreless at halftime, but the Browns exploded in the second half. They scored seventeen

points in the third quarter on a field goal and two Gary Collins touchdown receptions, then tacked on ten more fourth-quarter points for a convincing 27-0 victory. It was their first league title since 1955. Brown gained 114 yards on 27 carries—most coming in the second half.

It seemed as though the Browns could look forward to Jim Brown helping them win many more championships. But after the 1965 season, the thirty-year-old Brown shocked the football world by announcing his retirement, stating the football part of his life was over. Brown left pro football as the NFL's all-time leading rusher. It would take twenty years before Chicago's Walter Payton would break Brown's yardage record.

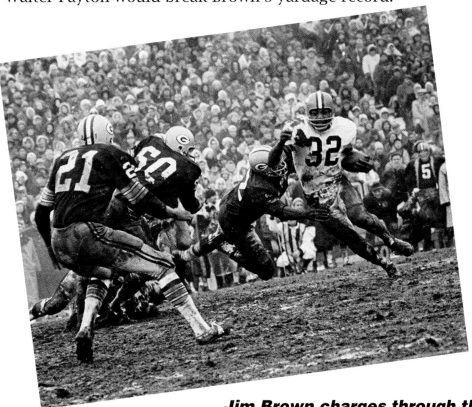

Jim Brown charges through the Green Bay defense.

The First Super Bowl

The NFL championship game was considered the ultimate professional football game. But starting in 1967, the matchup between the NFL champion and the AFL champion became the "Super Bowl."

On January 15, 1967, the Green Bay Packers became the first NFL team to play the AFL champions. Many experts considered the AFL an inferior league and did not give them much of a chance to win. In Super Bowl I, the Packers showed why the NFL was better when they soundly defeated the Kansas City Chiefs 35-10.

From the beginning, the Packers looked like they would roll to an easy victory. They scored in the first quarter after a long march down the field. It ended when Max McGee took a touchdown pass from Bart Starr, making the score 7-0.

But Kansas City refused to be intimidated. They tied the game in the second quarter on a Len Dawson touchdown pass. Predictions of a shutout quickly vanished. The Super Bowl was now a real game.

Jim Taylor put Green Bay back on top with a fourteen-yard run. But back came the Chiefs, as Dawson led his team down the field once again. The Packers defense stiffened, and Kansas City had to settle for a field goal. Still, the 14-10 halftime score was a shocker. It was anybody's game, and no one knew what to expect in the second half.

The Packers, however, quickly put to rest any hopes of a Kansas City upset. Green Bay's Willie Wood picked off a Dawson pass and returned it all the way to the Chiefs' five-yard line. Moments later, Elijah Pitts ran the ball in for a touchdown and a 21-10 score. The game was never the same.

Kansas City was shakened; the Packers were confident. Dawson found it difficult to even complete a pass, and the Chiefs' offense never threatened to score the remainder of the game. Green Bay added another third-quarter touchdown to make it 28-10, and the rout was on. A fourth-quarter touchdown by Pitts put the finishing touches on the game as Green Bay won the first-ever Super Bowl, 35-10.

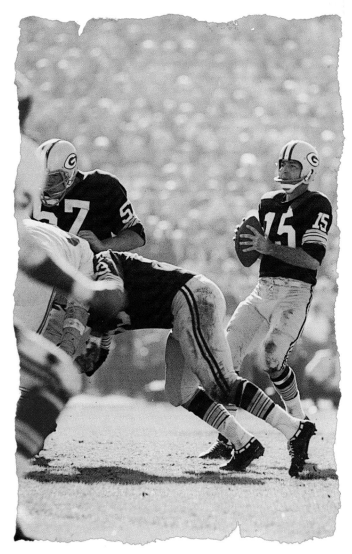

Quarterback Bart Starr of the Green Bay Packers.

The Ice Bowl

On December 31, 1967, the Green Bay Packers played the Dallas Cowboys for the NFL championship in a game that would be called "the Ice Bowl." The temperature on Lambeau Field was thirteen degrees below zero. The Cowboys wore gloves. But Packers' head coach Vince Lombardi would not allow his players the same luxury. "You've got to be bigger than the weather to be a winner," he told his gloveless team.

As the game wore on, the cold began to affect the Cowboys and their level of play. When Cowboys' wide receiver Bob Hayes was the intended receiver, he lined up with his hands out of his pants. When he was not the intended receiver, he lined up with his hands tucked in his waistband. The Packers' defense caught on to Hayes' peculiar habit and used it to their advantage.

Eventually the Packers found more flaws in the Dallas offense. Late in the game, the Packers made their last drive, starting from their own 31-yard line. They drove the length of the field and reached the Cowboys one-yard line. There were only a few seconds remaining. Dallas led 17-14.

Quarterback Bart Starr called a time-out and huddled with his teammates. They had noticed earlier that Jethro Pugh, the Cowboys' left tackle, charged too high on goal-line defense situations. So they knew a quarterback sneak would work. Lineman Jerry Kramer was confident he could block him. Rather

Packers' quarterback Bart Starr sneaks the ball over the goal line to beat the Dallas Cowboys in "the Ice Bowl."

than give the ball to the fullback and risk a fumble, the Packers just sneaked it in. The Packers had won the game 21-17. They were NFL champions for the third time in a row and the fifth time in seven years.

Repeat Champions

In 1968, the Green Bay Packers made it to the Super Bowl for the second year in a row. Once again, they showed that the NFL was superior to the AFL when they handled the Oakland Raiders 33-14.

Using their ball-control defense, the Packers turned a 16-7 halftime lead into a 33-14 rout on a Donny Anderson touchdown, a Chandler field goal, and Herb Adderley's interception return for another score. Oakland quarterback Daryle Lamonica threw a touchdown pass in the fourth quarter, making the final score 33-14. The Packers were the NFL's first back-to-back Super Bowl winners.

After the game was over, linemen Forrest Gregg and Jerry Kramer carried Lombardi from the field on their shoulders. Super Bowl II would be Lombardi's last game as head coach of the Green Bay Packers. "This," said Lombardi, "is the best way to leave a football field."

Opposite page:
Coach Vince Lombardi
after winning back-to-
back Super Bowls.

Joe Willie and the Jets

At the beginning of the 1968 season, the AFL's New York Jets were favored to make it to the Super Bowl. After all, they had one of pro football's best quarterbacks: Joe Willie Namath.

But the Jets were more than a one-man show. Emerson Boozer and Matt Snell were two of the best running backs in the league. And the defense, led by all-pro defensive back Johnny Sample and linebacker Al Atkinson, was one of the AFL's strongest.

The Jets did not disappoint their fans or themselves. They won the Eastern Division with an 11-3 record. And then they went on to beat the Western Division champion Oakland Raiders to advance to their first-ever Super Bowl.

Super Bowl III was more than just a championship game between two teams. It was a war between the AFL and the NFL. The National Football League did not respect teams from the AFL. They considered the American Football League as weak and second class. Even more, they thought the AFL would never win a Super Bowl. But the Jets did not see it that way. "Our team is better than any NFL team," Namath said. "We will win the Super Bowl. I guarantee it."

Few people listened to Namath's promise. The Baltimore Colts were eighteen-point favorites. Before the game, Colts' owner Carroll Rosenbloom prepared for the victory party. The

stage was set for one of the greatest upsets in professional football history.

The Jets knew they could beat the Colts. They studied films and saw weaknesses in the Colts' defense. Even more, they knew the Colts would key on Don Maynard. The Jets decided to make George Sauer the key to their offense.

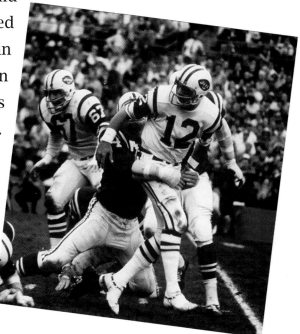

Joe Namath throws a pass against the Colts.

When the game began, the Jets shocked the Colts when Namath handed off to Snell who burst through the line for big yardage. Snell would have success the entire game. With their ground game in high gear, the Jets took command of the game.

As the Jets had predicted, Baltimore's defense keyed on Maynard. Sauer was often left alone, and he caught 8 passes for 133 yards. On the ground, Snell gained 121 yards on 30 carries as the Jets shocked the Colts 16-7. The AFL had finally won the respect they deserved.

Tom Dempsey and the Kick

Placekicker Tom Dempsey made NFL history in a game against the Detroit Lions on November 8, 1970. Dempsey entered the game with only two seconds remaining. The Saints had the ball on their own 45-yard line, and trailed Detroit by one point. That's when coach J. D. Roberts sent Dempsey in to attempt a 63-yard field goal. The crowd was silent. Though Dempsey had a strong leg, the NFL field goal record was fifty-six yards.

Dempsey was up to the challenge. He had succeeded in football despite being disabled. Dempsey had been born without a right hand and with only half a right foot. Teased by his peers, he was determined to show that he could compete with any athlete. He played tackle for his high school football team, and was good enough to sign to a professional contract while in junior college.

Holder Joe Scarpati took the snap and watched as Dempsey made his usual two-and-a-half-step run at the ball. Detroit's All-Pro lineman Alex Karras had a shot at blocking the kick, but he was too amused to give it his best effort.

Dempsey's mallet-like boot struck the ball with an unearthly thud. As Karras and his teammates looked on in shock, the

ball boomed towards the uprights, turning end-for-end. The crowd watched nervously, waiting for the ball to eventually fall short of its mark. But the ball kept climbing and climbing toward the goalpost.

Within moments, it became apparent that Dempsey's improbable kick just might have a chance. Now the crowd was breathless as the ball streaked for the goalpost. Just when the ball appeared to have lost its steam, it flew over the crossbar. The referee raised his hands, and Dempsey entered NFL history books for kicking the league's longest field goal. Even more, the field goal won the game. Dempsey was carried off the field by his teammates as the home crowd cheered wildly.

The Immaculate Reception

In Pittsburgh's first playoff game in 1972, the Steelers faced the Oakland Raiders. In a defensive battle at Pittsburgh, the Steelers trailed 7-6 with only 22 seconds remaining. Quarterback Terry Bradshaw had one play left. He called, "66 option." In the Raiders defensive huddle, defensive back Jack Tatum—the man they called "the Assassin"—readied himself for the final play. He was determined not to let the Steelers get past him.

From his own 40-yard line, Bradshaw took the snap, rolled to his right, and threw to running back John Fuqua. Just as the ball arrived, Tatum collided violently with Fuqua, and the ball flew fifteen yards backward to Pittsburgh running back Franco Harris, who was following the play.

As the ball fell toward the ground, Harris reached down and plucked the ball off his shoe tops. Tucking the ball under his arm, he rambled sixty yards and avoided one last Oakland defender to score the winning touchdown. The stadium erupted in celebration. Harris' "Immaculate Reception" was one of the most dramatic plays in the history of the NFL playoffs.

Franco Harris carries the ball.

Perfection

The 1972 season was a magical one for the Miami Dolphins. On offense, running backs Mercury Morris and Larry Csonka each rushed for more than one thousand yards—the first rushing duo to accomplish this feat. The Dolphins also had the NFL's number-one-rated defense known as the "No Name Defense" because they did not have well-known defensive stars. Even after starting quarterback Bob Griese broke his leg in the fifth game, backup quarterback Earl Morrall came on to lead the AFC in passing.

But the big story for the 1972 Dolphins was their record. They finished the season at 14-0, the first perfect season since the Chicago Bears racked up an 11-0 record in 1942.

The perfect Dolphins were favored to win their first Super Bowl. But in their first playoff game, Miami barely slipped by Cleveland 20-14. In the AFC championship game against the Steelers, the Dolphins struggled with Pittsburgh before finally winning 21-17.

Although the Dolphins were headed to the Super Bowl for the second straight year, they were considered underdogs to the Washington Redskins. One last game separated the Dolphins from perfection. They were not about to let their fans—or themselves—down.

Griese started for the Dolphins after missing twelve games and came out firing. Early in the game, he tossed a 28-yard touchdown pass to Howard Twilley as the Dolphins grabbed a 7-0 lead. Then the game settled into a defensive battle.

As time wore on, the Dolphins' defense intercepted two passes to stop Redskins' drives. When the game finally ended, Miami had a 14-7 victory. The Dolphins were still perfect—and they had won their first world championship. Don Shula called the 1972 Dolphins the finest team he had ever seen. Many historians and fans agree.

Don Shula coaches the Dolphins' perfect season.

The Steelers' 4th Super Bowl Win

In 1978, the Pittsburgh Steelers worked on their passing game and opened up their offense. The result was amazing as the Steelers finished with a 14-2 record, the best in the NFL. The "Steel Curtain" defense allowed the fewest points in the league. Quarterback Terry Bradshaw led the NFL in touchdown passes with twenty-eight.

In the playoffs, Pittsburgh destroyed Denver 33-10. Then in the AFC Championship, they tore apart the Houston Oilers 34-5. Going into their third Super Bowl, the Steelers looked invincible. But they were facing the defending Super Bowl champion Dallas Cowboys.

Bradshaw played the best game of his life. He passed for 318 yards and 4 touchdowns, and became the first quarterback ever to win 3 Super Bowls as the Steelers won 35-31.

One year later, the Steelers won their division, then pounded their way to a fourth Super Bowl appearance. The Steelers were heavily favored over the Los Angeles Rams, but the game was anything but easy.

Trailing 19-17 in the fourth quarter, the Steelers had the ball on their own 27-yard line. Bradshaw decided to go for the victory. He threw a long pass to John Stallworth. Stallworth

made the catch, and dashed seventy-three yards for the score. The Steelers were ahead 24-19.

A few minutes later, Bradshaw threw a 45-yard bomb to Stallworth that set up a 1-yard touchdown run by Franco Harris. The Steelers went on to win 31-19 and made football history with their fourth Super Bowl championship. Some experts called Pittsburgh "The Team of the '70s." Others called them "The Greatest Team Ever."

Pittsburgh quarterback Terry Bradshaw.

Plunkett and the Wild Card Raiders

In 1978, the Oakland Raiders failed to make the playoffs for the first time in seven years. To turn the club around, management hired Tom Flores as coach. He was expected to carry on the Raiders' winning tradition. Flores immediately turned to a misfit backup quarterback. His name was Jim Plunkett.

Plunkett had a few good seasons with the New England Patriots. But many experts thought he could not lead the Raiders to another championship.

Flores refused to give up on Plunkett. The quarterback responded by completing one of the greatest comebacks in NFL history.

The Raiders did not start well. They lost three of their first five games. Finally Plunkett led the Raiders to nine wins in the next eleven games. Their 11-5 record was good enough to make the playoffs as a wild card team.

It was an amazing comeback for both Plunkett and his team. But few observers gave the Raiders much of a chance to get to the Super Bowl—let alone win it. No wild card team had ever won an NFL championship. Oakland would have to play most of their playoff games on the road where it was difficult to win.

In their first playoff game in Oakland, the Raiders trounced Houston 27-7. Now it was off to frigid Cleveland to play the Browns. The Raiders scored a fourth-quarter touchdown to earn a 14-12 upset win and advance to the AFC title game in San Diego against the Chargers.

The Oakland defense proved that the Raiders belonged in the playoffs. They smothered San Diego's receivers and shut down the running game. Meanwhile, Plunkett and the offense built a 28-14 halftime lead. The Chargers mounted a furious comeback in the second half to make the score 28-24. But the Oakland defense stiffened, and San Diego would get no closer. For the first time in NFL history, a wild card team had reached the Super Bowl.

Despite their accomplishment, the Raiders remained big underdogs against the NFC's Philadelphia Eagles. But once again, the Raiders bucked tradition. Lester Hayes and the defense clamped down on the Eagles' offense as Oakland stunned the NFL with a 27-10 victory. Plunkett threw three touchdown passes—including a Super Bowl record eighty-yard bomb to fullback Kenny King. For his efforts, Plunkett was named the game's MVP. His remarkable comeback was now complete. And the Raiders had beaten the odds. They were the first wild card team to win the Super Bowl.

The Catch

In the 1981 season, the San Francisco 49ers and their young quarterback, Joe Montana, were looking for their first Super Bowl appearance. The 49ers were playing well, but they had to get past the Dallas Cowboys in the January 1982 NFC championship game.

The Cowboys took a 17-14 halftime lead. But the 49ers came back in the third quarter with a touchdown to jump ahead 21-17.

In the fourth quarter, the Cowboys kicked a field goal, then scored a touchdown for a 27-21 lead. With just five minutes remaining in the game, the 49ers began a long drive from their own ten-yard line. Montana moved his team down the field with pinpoint passes and timely scrambles. He drove the 49ers all the way to the six-yard line.

On third down, Montana rolled to his right to avoid the Dallas pass rush. Montana saw Dwight Clark cutting across the back of the end zone. He lofted a pass in Clark's direction. Clark leaped high in the air and came down with the ball for the score. "The Catch," as it was known, propelled the 49ers to a 28-27 win and their first Super Bowl berth.

Opposite page: Dwight Clark makes "The Catch."

The Records Fall

There may never be another year in NFL history like 1984. That year, many all-time records were set—records that may never be surpassed.

Dan Marino of the Miami Dolphins set a single-season passing record with 5,084 yards and 48 touchdowns. Eric Dickerson of the Los Angeles Rams broke O.J. Simpson's single-season rushing record when he ran for 2,105 yards. And wide receiver Art Monk of the Washington Redskins caught 106 passes, setting a new mark for most receptions in one season.

Perhaps most impressive was the record set by Walter Payton of the Chicago Bears. He broke Jim Brown's career rushing mark of 12,312, finishing the season with 13,309 career rushing yards.

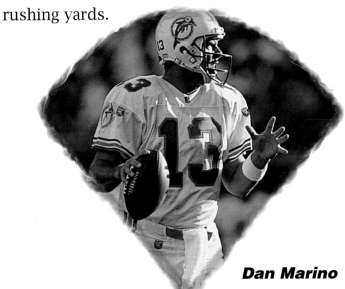

Dan Marino

Walter Payton

The Drive

Nearly 80,000 fans watched the Cleveland Browns and Denver Broncos battle to a 10-10 halftime tie in the 1987 AFC Championship game. Rich Karlis kicked a 26-yard field goal for the only score in the third quarter. Early in the fourth quarter, Cleveland tied the game with a field goal. With less than six minutes remaining, Cleveland went ahead 20-13.

On the next kickoff, the Broncos' Gene Lang fumbled the ball before recovering at the Denver two-yard line. The Broncos were ninety-eight yards away from the tying touchdown.

Quarterback John Elway calmly led the Broncos on their longest drive of the game. With 1:48 remaining, he faced a 3rd-and-18 at the Cleveland 48. A twenty-yard pass to Mark Jackson kept "The Drive" alive. Five plays later, Elway found Jackson in the end zone and sent the game into overtime.

Cleveland took the overtime kickoff but could not move the ball. Then Elway led the Broncos on another long drive. With 5:48 gone, Karlis lined up for a field goal at the Browns' 23-yard line. His kick curved left—but went through the uprights. The Broncos were AFC champions.

Opposite page: Rich Karlis kicking a field goal.

Super Blowout

In 1989, Bill Walsh quit as head coach of the San Francisco 49ers and moved into the broadcast booth. Fans wondered if the team would continue their winning ways. Defensive coordinator George Seifert became the new head coach, and the 49ers kept on rolling.

Quarterback Joe Montana had his best season ever. He set a new NFL mark with a 112.4 passing rating. Wide receiver Jerry Rice broke the team record for touchdown catches in only his fifth season. Roger Craig rushed for over one thousand yards, and the defense played well despite losing free safety Jeff Fuller to a career-ending injury. The 49ers' 14-2 record was the best in the NFL.

In the first round of the playoffs, San Francisco easily defeated the Minnesota Vikings 41-13. In the NFC championship game, the 49ers rolled over the Rams. Montana passed for 262 yards and two touchdowns, completing 26-of-30 passes. The 49ers seized a 21-3 halftime lead and coasted to a 30-3 win. Now they had a chance to repeat as Super Bowl champions.

It was the best Super Bowl ever—for the 49ers. Montana and San Francisco made football history with their fourth championship of the decade. They also became the first back-to-back winner since the Steelers of the 1970s. Their 55-10 victory over the Denver Broncos was the biggest margin in Super Bowl history—and the most points scored by a Super Bowl team.

Jerry Rice caught 7 passes for 148 yards and 3 touchdowns. Montana was 22 of 29 for 297 yards and 5 touchdowns. At one point, he completed thirteen consecutive passes. His efforts earned him his third Super Bowl MVP award.

49ers receiver Jerry Rice.

The Rally

Though they had played in the Super Bowl the previous season, the Buffalo Bills failed to win the AFC East crown in 1992. But it was still a successful year as they finished 11-5. The defense improved, and running back Thurman Thomas led the league in total yards for the fourth straight year, breaking Jim Brown's record. Few experts, however, thought the Bills would return to the Super Bowl.

In the first round of the playoffs, Buffalo faced the Houston Oilers without quarterback Jim Kelly, who was injured. Houston had a high-powered offense, led by quarterback Warren Moon. They exploded for twenty-one second-quarter points and took a seemingly unbeatable 28-3 halftime lead. Houston added to their lead in the third quarter on a 58-yard interception return for a touchdown. Buffalo's long playoff run seemed ready to end.

But then a miracle happened. Kelly's replacement, Frank Reich, led Buffalo to 4 third-quarter touchdowns—including 3 touchdown passes which brought the Bills to within 35-31.

Buffalo took the lead 38-35 in the fourth quarter on another Reich touchdown pass. But Houston managed to rally for a game-tying field goal that sent the game into overtime. Reich directed another drive that set up Steve Christie's game-winning 32-yard field goal. It was a miraculous win—the biggest come-from-behind victory in NFL history.

Quarterback Frank Reich.

Shula Surpasses Halas

Miami head coach Don Shula began the 1993 season saying he wanted the coaching record for most career victories to come in a season in which the Dolphins achieved success. But that didn't happen. With a 9-2 record on Thanksgiving Day, the Dolphins had the best record in the NFL. Then they lost their final five games to miss the playoffs.

Quarterback Dan Marino, who hadn't missed a game in eight years, suffered a torn Achilles tendon in the fifth game and was gone. Scott Mitchell took over and was the NFL's Player of the Month of October. Then he too was injured. That left rookie Doug Pederson and Steve DeBerg in charge until Mitchell returned. But the Dolphins could not overcome Marino's loss.

Despite the disappointing season, Shula could finally celebrate his personal accomplishments. Shula got his 325th victory on November 14 to break George Halas' record of 324 career wins.

Opposite page: Don Shula surpasses Halas' victory record with 325 wins.

Steve Young
Makes History

In 1993, 49ers' quarterback Steve Young ran wild over his opponents. He became the first player in NFL history to lead the league in passing three straight years. Ricky Watters rushed for 950 yards and scored 11 touchdowns. Jerry Rice caught 98 passes for 1,503 yards and 15 touchdowns.

The 49ers set a club record with 6,435 yards on offense and scored 473 points—29.6 per game—just 2 points shy of the team record. San Francisco shook off a 3-3 start to win its 10th divisional title in 13 years and extended a league record of 11 seasons with 10 or more victories.

Opposite page:
San Francisco quarterback
Steve Young.

The 49ers' Fifth Super Bowl Win

In 1994, San Francisco 49ers' quarterback Steve Young had impressive passing statistics. But everyone wondered if he could win the big game like Joe Montana did in his years with the team. The pressure was on Young to win an NFL-record fifth Super Bowl title for San Francisco.

Young responded to the pressure by guiding the 49ers to a 44-14 win on opening day against the Raiders. But in Week 2 against Montana and the Chiefs, Young came up short, 24-17. San Francisco then won 2 in a row before being embarrassed 40-8 by the Philadelphia Eagles.

That was the turning point for Young and the 49ers. They reeled off 5 straight wins—including a 21-14 victory over the defending champion Dallas Cowboys.

The 49ers won another 5 in a row to bring the streak to 10 before dropping a Week 17 game to the Vikings. The game was meaningless, since the 49ers had already clinched home field advantage throughout the playoffs.

In the NFC divisional playoff against Chicago, the 49ers rolled to a 30-3 halftime lead and routed the Bears 44-15. In the NFC Championship game, the team of the 1980s earned a trip to the Super Bowl in 1995 by beating Dallas.

The 49ers streaked to a 21-0 lead halfway through the first quarter.   The 49ers then answered every challenge by the Cowboys to put away the champs 38-28. Steve Young was one win away from his first championship.

Super Bowl XXIX was one-sided. The 49ers scored touchdowns on their first 3 possessions and led 28-10 at halftime. By the end of the third quarter, it was 42-18. The 49ers and Chargers traded scores in the fourth quarter for a 49-26 San Francisco win.

In the game, Young threw a Super Bowl record six touchdowns and became the second player in as many years to follow an MVP regular season by winning the same award in the Super Bowl. Young was also the game's leading rusher with forty-nine yards on five carries.

With the victory, the 49ers became the first team in NFL history to win five Super Bowls.

Steve Young celebrates a touchdown.

Emmitt Smith: Touchdown Leader

On December 25, 1995, Dallas running back Emmitt Smith set the single-season NFL record for rushing and total touchdowns as the Cowboys cruised to a 37-13 victory over the Arizona Cardinals. With the win, Dallas wrapped up home-field advantage throughout the NFC playoffs, finishing one game ahead of San Francisco and Green Bay.

Smith scored on a three-yard run with 5:49 to play in the game for his 25th touchdown of the season, bettering the mark of 24 set by John Riggins of the Washington Redskins in 1983. It was also Smith's 100th career touchdown, making him the 10th player in league history to reach that level.

Smith also captured his fourth NFL rushing title with 1,773 yards and set a franchise record with 377 carries, bettering his mark of 373 set in 1992. He also set a career high in rushing yards, surpassing his personal best of 1,713 yards in 1992.

Opposite page:
Touchdown leader
Emmitt Smith.

The NFL's All-Time Leading Passer

In 1995, Miami Dolphins' star quarterback Dan Marino continued his march into the Hall of Fame as he broke Fran Tarkenton's record and became the National Football League's all-time passing yardage leader.

Marino eclipsed Tarkenton, who passed for 47,003 yards for the Minnesota Vikings and New York Giants from 1961 to 1978, in the first quarter of a game against the New England Patriots with a 10-yard pass to Irving Fryar. Marino finished with 333 yards for a total of 47,299 yards in his career.

"It's nice," Marino said. "I really appreciate the fans' support. Breaking Fran's record as the all-time leading passer is special to me."

Marino noted some of the receivers who had helped him become the most prolific passer in league history.

"I just had the opportunity to see (Mark) Duper and (Mark) Clayton, who were at the game," he said. "Those guys were a big part of that record, along with a lot of other players and teammates, and the fans who supported me."

Marino already had broken Tarkenton's career completions record on October 8, 1995.

Entering the 1995 season, his thirteenth with the Dolphins, Marino was already the owner of twenty NFL records and tied for six others. He ranked third all-time in passing efficiency, behind Steve Young and Joe Montana.

Marino eventually broke another of Tarkenton's records, throwing 4 touchdown passes to snap a tie with the former Vikings star and give him 346 for his career.

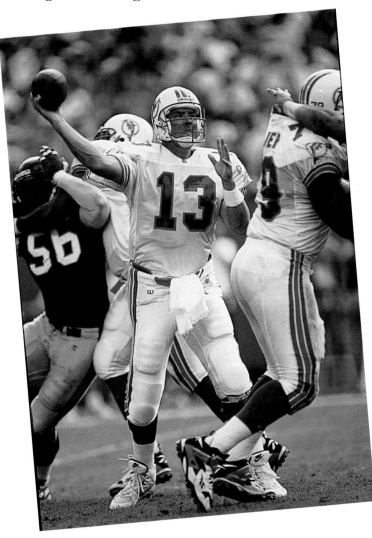

Dan Marino surpasses Fran Tarkenton to become the NFL's all-time leading passer.

Cooking With Rice

In 1995, San Francisco 49ers' superstar Jerry Rice, regarded by many to be the greatest wide receiver in NFL history, became the all-time leader in receiving yardage.

Rice needed just 2 quarters in a game against the New Orleans Saints to surpass the 73 yards receiving he needed to move past the 14,004 receiving yards amassed by James Lofton from 1978 to 1993. Rice had 8 catches for 108 yards, giving him 14,040 career yards in 10.5 seasons.

Rice became the all-time leader when he caught a thirteen-yard pass from Elvis Grbac in the second quarter for his sixth reception of the game. Rice received a standing ovation from the fans after the historic catch.

"It was great breaking the record," Rice said. "I would like to thank all the guys who put me in this position."

Rice, who was in his 11th season with the 49ers, had 877 catches for 14,040 yards and an NFL record 148 touchdowns, 9 on running plays. His 139 receiving touchdowns were the most in NFL history.

Rice, who turned thirty-three on October 13th, had never missed a game in his NFL career, not including three replacement games in 1987. He had made 9 straight appearances as a Pro Bowl starter and recorded an NFL record 9 consecutive 1,000-yard seasons. Rice passed Jim Brown's record of 126 touchdowns during the 1994 season.

San Francisco 49ers'
wide receiver Jerry Rice.

The Team of the '90s

Entering the 1995 NFL season, the Dallas Cowboys had an NFL-best twenty consecutive winning seasons from 1966 to 1985, and a record number of Super Bowl appearances (seven). Even more impressive, they were the only team to win more than one Super Bowl in two different decades (1970s and 1990s), and were winners of two of the last three Super Bowls as well as three consecutive NFC Eastern Division titles. With the addition of cornerback Deion Sanders, the Cowboys were favored to unseat the San Francisco 49ers as Super Bowl champions.

Dallas responded to the pressure by finishing with a 12-4 record, good for first place in the NFC Eastern Division. In the playoffs, they easily defeated the Philadelphia Eagles 30-11 before handling the Green Bay Packers 38-27 in the NFC Championship game to earn a record 8th Super Bowl appearance.

The Cowboys were big favorites over the Pittsburgh Steelers in Super Bowl XXX. Dallas jumped out to a 13-0 first half lead with two Chris Boniol field goals and a 3-yard touchdown pass from Troy Aikman to Jay Novacek. But the Steelers scored a touchdown late in the second quarter to cut the deficit to 13-7 at the half.

Cowboy cornerback Larry Brown snagged his first interception early in the third quarter, returning an errant Neil

O'Donnell pass 44 yards to the Steelers 18-yard line. After a 17-yard completion to Michael Irvin, Smith carried it over from one yard out to stake Dallas to a 20-7 cushion.

Pittsburgh recovered a surprise onside kick after Neil Johnson banged a 46-yard field goal through the uprights. Five straight O'Donnell completions set up Bam Morris for a one-yard touchdown run and had the Steelers thinking upset.

After Dallas was forced to punt, Pittsburgh took over at their own 32 with 4:15 to play and trailing by only 3. But O'Donnell's pass was intercepted by Brown and returned thirty-three yards to the Pittsburgh six-yard line. Smith carried it in over right tackle from 4 yards out for the 27-17 win. The touchdown was Smith's eighteenth postseason touchdown, tying Thurman Thomas for the NFL postseason record. Brown was named MVP of the contest, the first defensive MVP since Richard Dent of the Chicago Bears in Super Bowl XX.

With their third Super Bowl victory in the last four years, the Cowboys joined San Francisco as the only teams with five Super Bowl wins, earning them praise from football experts who called them "The Team of the '90s."

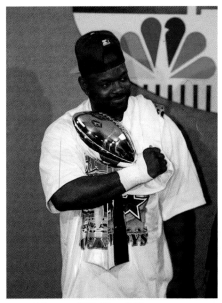

Emmitt Smith celebrates another Super Bowl victory.

More Unforgettable Moments

1929—Chicago Cardinals' Ernie Nevers scores six touchdowns in one game.

1932—The Chicago Bears give up only forty-four points in one season.

1934—The Chicago Bears record their seventeenth consecutive victory.

1939—Pittsburgh's Frank Filchock throws a 99-yard pass to Andy Farkas.

Ernie Nevers of the Chicago Cardinals.

1943—Chicago's Sid Luckman throws seven touchdown passes in one game.

1945—Green Bay scores forty-one points in one quarter.

1949—Pittsburgh's Bob Gage runs for ninety-seven yards on one play.

1951—The Rams' Norm Van Brocklin gains 554 yards passing in 1 game.

1952—Detroit's Pat Harder scores nineteen points in one playoff game.

1960—Green Bay's Paul Hornung scores 176 points in 1 season.

1963—Oakland's Daryle Lamonica throws a 93-yard touchdown pass in the playoffs.

1965—Cleveland Browns' running back Jim Brown scores his 126th career touchdown—an NFL record.

1965—Chicago Bears' running back Gale Sayers scores six touchdowns in one game.

1965—Baltimore's Lenny Moore scores a touchdown in his eighteenth consecutive game.

1967—St. Louis placekicker Jim Bakken kicks seven field goals in one game.

1967—Green Bay's Travis Williams averages 41.1 yards per kickoff return in 1 season.

1968—Green Bay's Don Chandler kicks four field goals in the Super Bowl.

1968—Jim Turner of the N.Y. Jets kicks thirty-four field goals in one season.

1969—Steve O'Neal of the New York Jets kicks a 98-yard punt.

1969—Oakland's Daryle Lamonica throws six touchdown passes in one playoff game.

1970—Minnesota's Fred Cox kicks a field goal in his thirty-first consecutive game.

1974—Miami wins its twenty-seventh consecutive home game.

1975—Oakland Raiders' placekicker George Blanda plays in his NFL-record twenty-sixth season.

Fred Cox kicking a field goal.

1975—Buffalo's O.J. Simpson scores twenty-three touchdowns in one season.

1977—Chicago's Walter Payton rushes for 275 yards in 1 game.

1978—New England rushes for 3,165 yards in 1 season.

1979—Minnesota Vikings' defensive lineman Jim Marshall plays in his 282nd consecutive NFL game.

1979—St. Louis' Roy Green returns a kickoff 106 yards for a touchdown.

Jim Marshall stopping the rush.

1979—Minnesota's Paul Krause intercepts his eighty-first career pass.

1979—Houston's Vernon Perry intercepts four passes in one playoff game.

1980—Houston's Earl Campbell rushes for 200+ yards 4 times; also records 1,934 rushing yards for the season.

1981—San Diego's Kellen Winslow catches thirteen passes in one playoff game.

1981—Oakland's Rod Martin intercepts three passes in the Super Bowl.

1982—Cincinnati's Dan Ross catches eleven passes in the Super Bowl.

1983—Dallas' Tony Dorsett scores on a 99-yard touchdown run.

1983—The Rams' Eric Dickerson sets the rookie rushing record with 1,808 yards and scores 18 touchdowns.

Eric Dickerson running hard.

1983—New York Giants' placekicker Ali Haji-Sheikh kicks his thirty-fifth field goal of the season.

1983—The Washington Redskins score 541 points for the season.

1983—John Riggins sets the NFL record with twenty-four touchdowns, all on the ground, for the Washington Redskins.

1984—The Chicago Bears record seventy-two sacks in one season.

1984—Mark Gastineau of the New York Jets records his twenty-second sack of the season.

1984—Miami scores seventy touchdowns in one season.

1984—Cleveland's Steve Cox kicks a sixty-yard field goal.

1984—The San Francisco 49ers record their fifteenth win of the season in the Super Bowl.

1984—The Raiders' Marcus Allen scores on a 74-yard touchdown run in the Super Bowl.

1985—The Rams' Ron Brown returns two kickoffs for touchdowns in one game.

1985—Minnesota placekicker Jan Stenerud kicks his 373rd career field goal.

1985—The Rams' Eric Dickerson rushes for 248 yards in a playoff game.

1985—Miami's Don Shula coaches in his sixth Super Bowl.

1985—San Francisco's Roger Craig scores eighteen points in the Super Bowl.

1986—Cleveland's Bernie Kosar throws for 489 yards in a playoff game.

1986—The Chicago Bears record seven sacks in the Super Bowl.

1987—Philadelphia's John Teltschik punts fifteen times in one game.

1987—Chicago's Walter Payton sets an NFL record for most rushing yards in a career with 16,726.

1987—Minnesota's Chuck Nelson kicks five field goals in one playoff game.

1987—Anthony Carter of the Minnesota Vikings has 227 receiving yards in one playoff game.

1988—San Francisco's Roger Craig scores on an eighty-yard touchdown run in the playoffs.

1988—Washington's Timmy Smith rushes for 204 yards in the Super Bowl.

1988—Washington's Doug Williams throws an eighty-yard touchdown pass in the Super Bowl.

1989—Minnesota's Rich Karlis kicks seven field goals in one game.

1989—The Rams' Flipper Anderson gains 336 receiving yards in 1 game.

1989—San Francisco's Joe Montana throws for 357 yards and Jerry Rice has 215 receiving yards in the Super Bowl.

A lethal combination: Rice and Montana.

1990—The 49ers' Jerry Rice catches five touchdown passes in one game.

1990—Miami's Pete Stoyanovich kicks a 58-yard field goal in a playoff game.

1991—The Saints' Morten Andersen kicks a sixty-yard field goal.

1992—Washington's Art Monk catches his 847th career pass.

Art Monk heading for the end zone.

1992—The Giants' Lawrence Taylor records his 126th career sack.

1992—Houston's Warren Moon completes thirty-six passes in a playoff game.

1993—The Raiders' Jeff Jaeger kicks thirty-five field goals in one season.

1993—Green Bay's Sterling Sharpe catches 112 passes in 1 season.

1993—San Francisco's Ricky Watters scores thirty points in one playoff game.

1994—San Diego's John Carney kicks thirty-four field goals in one season.

1994—Minnesota's Cris Carter catches 122 passes in 1 season.

1994—Minnesota's Fuad Reveiz kicks thirty-four field goals in one season.

1994—New England's Drew Bledsoe completes forty-five passes in one game.

Index